ANNE OF GREEN GABLES

Comprehension Guide
by Ned Bustard

veritas
PRESS

This guide is dedicated
with affection to
Anne (with-an-E) Symons,
whose mother read
this lovely book
to young Anne
one summer,
in the hot afternoons,
resting on her bed,
so many years ago
on the family farm in
Townsend, Delaware.

First Edition 2009

Copyright ©2009 Veritas Press
www.VeritasPress.com
ISBN 978-1-932168-79-2

Printed in the United States of America.

ANNE OF GREEN GABLES
How to use this Guide

This guide is intended to help you study, understand and enjoy *Anne of Green Gables*. You might ask if a guide is really necessary to read a book. Is the student not just working to improve reading skills while being taught to enjoy reading a book? Certainly it is the case that the more a child reads, the more he should improve his skills, but quantity is not the only issue. Once a child has received adequate phonetic training he should learn how to read a book. Most educators using this guide will be teaching children in the grammar stage, generally understood to be during the elementary years in a classical education. (For a thorough understanding of classical Christian education we recommend reading *Recovering the Lost Tools of Learning or The Case for Classical Christian Education,* both by Douglas Wilson.) The basic goals of reading in the grammar stage are as follows:

The student should be able to:
1. Fluently read a given selection orally.
2. Show an increased desire for reading.
3. Show comprehension on a literal and inferential level.
4. Demonstrate an increased vocabulary.
5. Identify basic biblical values in the literature being read.
6. Identify various styles (myths, poems, fantasy, fiction, nonfiction, etc.)

Answers to the questions are found in the back of the guide. Although the answers in the guide appear in an abbreviated form, the students' answers should be in complete sentences, and they should restate the question in their answer.

Example:

Question: What did Anne name the geranium?
Answer: Anne named the geranium "Bonny."

Such writing practice trains the student to answer thoroughly, completely and with proper grammar. Another reason is to encourage integration. We want students to understand that how they write something is as important as what they write.

You may wonder how to grade the student's work in this guide. Keep it simple. Unless otherwise indicated you should assume that each question is worth five points.

ANNE OF GREEN GABLES
Mrs. Rachel Lynde Is Surprised

1. What was the effect of Mrs. Rachel Lynde on the intricate, headlong brook from the old Cuthbert place?

   _____

   _____

   _____

2. Mrs. Rachel Lynde was a notable housewife, ran the Sewing Circle, helped run the Sunday-school, and was the strongest prop of the Church Aid Society and Foreign Missions Auxiliary. But what was it that she had done that awed the Avonlea housekeepers?

   _____

   _____

   _____

3. What puzzled Mrs. Lynde at half past three that afternoon?

   _____

   _____

   _____

4. What kept the kitchen at Green Gables from being cheerful?

   _____

   _____

   _____

5. In addition to being slightly distrustful of sunshine, describe Marilla.

   _____

   _____

   _____

   _____

6. What unexpected news jolted Mrs. Rachel into thinking in exclamation points?

_____

_____

_____

7. What "Job's comforting" did Rachel offer to Marilla?

_____

_____

_____

ANNE OF GREEN GABLES
Matthew Cuthbert is Surprised

1. Who were the only mysterious creatures who Matthew did not dread?

   _____

   _____

2. Describe Matthew's appearance.

   _____

   _____

   _____

3. What did Matthew feel was harder than bearding a lion in its den?

   _____

   _____

4. Describe the appearance of the girl.

   _____

   _____

   _____

5. What were the little girl's plans for the night if Matthew did not arrive?

   _____

   _____

6. According to the freckled witch, what was it easy to be without knowing it?

   _____

   _____

   _____

7. Who does Matthew's companion think is the only person who she'd have a chance to marry?

_____

_____

_____

8. Why couldn't the orphan girl feel exactly perfectly happy?

_____

_____

_____

9. What caused the little chatterbox to suddenly stop talking?

_____

_____

10. What is the actual name of the Lake of Shining Waters?

_____

ANNE OF GREEN GABLES
Project—Pure Contour Nature Drawing

Throughout this book Nature plays an important part. From the very start the beautiful trees and natural sights of Avonlea are glorified. Nature is a companion, a comfort, and a metaphor for Faith and the future. Pay attention to all the ways the author weaves God's Creation into the story and the significance it has on the narrative. To help you look at Nature with imagination and fresh appreciation that Anne displays, try this project.

First find a subject with a lot of details. Perhaps it is a tree outside your window, a floral arrangment on the table or even just a leaf. Then tape a piece of paper on a table. Sit so your drawing hand, holding the pencil, is ready to draw on the taped-down paper, but turn away from the paper, looking at the object you are drawing. During the time you spend drawing, you may *not* look at the paper.

Draw very, very slowly, without lifting the point of the pencil from the paper, following every nook and cranny of the object. Draw only clearly defined edges, resisting the temptation to color in shadows. Draw very, very slowly as you move your pencil, moving your eyes along the edge of the object you are using for your subject matter. Imagine that the pupil of your eye is the lead of the pencil. Don't look at your paper!

When you are all done, see how well you saw. The proportions of the drawing will be all wrong—that is okay. What you want to see is whether you recorded with your pencil every detail that your eye picked up.

Go back and try this exercise a few more times, then try it again but allow yourself to look three times. Finally draw it again, looking at the paper and the object and see how well you can apply your powers of observation to the final drawing.

ANNE OF GREEN GABLES
Marilla Cuthbert is Surprised and *Morning at Green Gables*

1. Why did Matthew not introduce their guest to Marrilla by name?

   _____

   _____

   _____

2. Who was Cordelia?

   _____

   _____

3. Under what circumstances could Anne reconcile herself with name?

   _____

   _____

   _____

4. Why couldn't Anne eat the crab-apple preserve?

   _____

   _____

   _____

5. Describe the rigid east gable room.

   _____

   _____

   _____

   _____

6. How could Marilla tell that Matthew was perturbed?

   _____

   _____

   _____

7. What did Marilla instruct Anne to do the following morning which she forgot?

    _____

    _____

    _____

    _____

8. What did Marilla order Anne to do which ended up making Marilla uncomfortable?

    _____

    _____

    _____

    _____

9. What did Anne name the geranium?

    _____

    _____

ANNE OF GREEN GABLES
Anne's History and *Marilla Makes Up Her Mind*

1. Summarize Anne's history—the *real* one, not the one she wanted to tell Marilla.

_____

_____

_____

_____

_____

_____

_____

_____

_____

_____

_____

_____

_____

_____

_____

_____

_____

_____

2. Why did Mrs. Spencer think Anne wouldn't need to return to the orphanage?

_____

_____

_____

3. After meeting Mrs. Blewett, how did Marilla change her story about the reason she had come that day?

    _____

    _____

    _____

    _____

    _____

    _____

4. What conditions did Marilla set for what they would do with Anne?

    _____

    _____

    _____

    _____

    _____

    _____

5. How did Matthew amend her conditions?

    _____

    _____

    _____

    _____

ANNE OF GREEN GABLES
Anne Says Her Prayers and *Anne's Bringing-up Is Begun*

1. *Fill in the blank.* God is a spirit, _____, _____ and

   _____, in His being, wisdom, power, holiness, justice,

   _____, and _____.

2. What did Anne like about learning the catechism?

   _____

   _____

   _____

3. Why did Anne dislike God?

   _____

   _____

   _____

4. Instead of *"Now I lay me down to sleep, I pray the Lord my soul to keep; Should I die
   before I wake, I pray the Lord my soul to take,"* how did Marilla teach Anne to pray?

   _____

   _____

   _____

5. What did Anne ask God for, and how did she end her prayer?

   _____

   _____

   _____

6. What was Anne's reaction to the news that she was going to be allowed to stay at Green
   Gables?

   _____

   _____

7. What did Anne want to call Marilla instead of "Miss Cuthbert"?

_____

_____

_____

8. Instead of obeying Marilla right away and getting the illustrated card that was on the mantelpiece, what did Anne do?

_____

_____

_____

9. Anne was captivated by a chromolithograph called "Christ Blessing Little Children." What idea about the artwork did Anne share which Marilla considered "positively irreverent"?

_____

_____

_____

_____

10. What kind of friend does Anne dream of finding in Avonlea?

_____

_____

11. In what way was Marilla like the Duchess in *Alice in Wonderland?*

_____

_____

_____

12. Who was Katie Maurice?

_____

_____

ANNE OF GREEN GABLES
Project—Marilla's Morals

"Diana is a very pretty little girl. She has black eyes and hair and rosy cheeks. And she is good and smart, which is better than being pretty."

Marilla was as fond of morals as the Duchess in Wonderland, and was firmly convinced that one should be tacked on to every remark made to a child who was being brought up.

But Anne waved the moral inconsequently aside and seized only on the delightful possibilities before it.

While reading Anne of Green Gables, *keep track of all of the "morals" that Marilla tries to teach Anne, or just color the picture of the Duchess and Alice below.*

"Tut, tut, child! Everything's got a moral, if only you can find it."

ANNE OF GREEN GABLES
Mrs. Rachel Lynde Is Properly Horrified and *Anne's Apology*

1. At what point would Marilla quench Anne's descriptions of her voyages of exploration?

_____

_____

_____

2. Why did Anne call Mrs. Lynde "a rude, impolite, unfeeling woman"?

_____

_____

_____

3. Instead of a fair-sized birch switch, what discipline did Marilla use with Anne?

_____

_____

_____

4. Why was Marilla as angry with herself as with Anne?

_____

_____

_____

5. Before visiting Anne, when was the last time Matthew had been upstairs?

_____

_____

_____

6. Quivering in mournful penitence Anne apologized to Mrs. Lynde. What did Mrs. Lynde say in response that caused Anne to view her as a benefactor?

_____

_____

_____

7. Why did Anne erroneously think that she was not guilty of the sin of vanity?

_____

_____

_____

8. What caused a throb of the maternity to well up in Marilla's heart?

_____

_____

_____

9. What theological insight did Anne have in response to Marilla's moralistic instruction that "you should never find it hard to say your prayers?"

_____

_____

_____

ANNE OF GREEN GABLES

Anne's Impressions of Sunday-School and
A Solemn Vow and Promise

1. Why didn't Marilla make pretty dresses for Anne?

   _____

   _____

   _____

2. Why didn't Marilla go to Sunday-school with Anne?

   _____

   _____

3. How did the girls at the church treat Anne?

   _____

   _____

   _____

4. While Mr. Bell prayed in a disinterested way to a God who was very far off, what did Anne pray?

   _____

   _____

   _____

5. Why was Marilla hampered in reproving Anne for the things Anne had said, especially about the minister's sermons and Mr. Bell's prayers?

   _____

   _____

   _____

6. What reasons did Anne give for thinking that putting buttercups and wild roses on her hat was acceptable?

    _____

    _____

    _____

7. Anne was frightened that Diana Barry wouldn't like her, but according to Marilla, what should Anne have been concerned about instead?

    _____

    _____

    _____

8. Why was Mrs. Barry glad at the prospect of a playmate for Diana?

    _____

    _____

    _____

9. To complete their oath to be faithful bosom friends as long as the sun and moon shall endure, what were Anne and Diana forced to imagine?

    _____

    _____

    _____

10. What was Diana going to give to Anne and what was Anne (thanks to Matthew) going to give to Diana?

    _____

    _____

    _____

    _____

ANNE OF GREEN GABLES
Project 1—A Wholesome Sweet

Ingredients

powdered sugar

1 cup granulated sugar

1 cup light corn syrup

1 cup water

1/2 tsp. peppermint oil

candy thermometer

Directions

Sprinkle a thick coat of powdered sugar on a cookie sheet. Then combine the granulated sugar, light corn syrup and water in a heavy saucepan. Cook over medium-high heat until the hard-crack stage on a candy thermometer. Remove from heat. Add the peppermint oil. Stir well. Pour onto the cookie sheet. Sprinkle with more powdered sugar. Cut with kitchen shears as soon as cool enough to handle. Store in an airtight container or freezer bag.

ANNE OF GREEN GABLES
Project 2—Flower Drawings

There are many flowers identified in this chapter. Below you will find a list of some that are mentioned in this chapter as well as a partial list of other flowers referenced. *Choose a few to research and draw them in the booklet you make from the following directions..*

Flower Drawing Book

To make this six-page booklet, fold the next page along all the dotted lines then unfold. Fold the page in half vertically and cut along the solid center line, then unfold. Fold the page in half horizontally, then holding on to each side, gently push the ends together to form the pages of the book. Fold the front and back covers around so that the corners meet. Crease well.

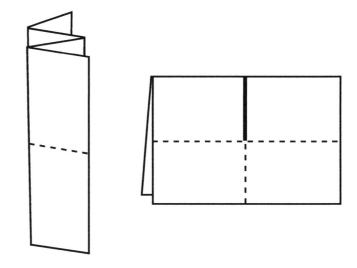

THE BARRYS' GARDEN FLOWERS
Bleeding hearts *(Dicentra spectabilis)*
Crimson peonies *(Paeonia officinalis)*
Scotch roses *(Rosa spinosissima)*
Columbines *(Aquilegia vulgaris)*
Bouncing Bets *(Saponaria officinals)*
Adam-and-Eve *(Aplectrum hyemale)*
Rice Lilies *(Maianthemum canadense)*

OTHERS FLOWERS IN THE BOOK
Ladies' Eardrops *(Impatiens capensis)*
Junebells *(Linnea Borealis)*
Geranium *(Pelargonium)*
Mayflowers *(Epigaea repens)*
June lilies *(Narcissus)*
Starfloweres *(Trientalis borealis)*
Pigeon Berries *(Phylotacca americana)*
Honeysuckle *(Lonicera Periclymenum)*
Joe-Pye Weed (thistles) *(Eupatorium)*
Hollyhocks *(Althaea rosea)*

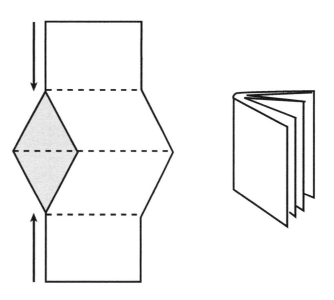

The Flora of AVONLEA

ANNE OF GREEN GABLES
The Delights of Anticipation and *Anne's Confession*

1. What aspect of the upcoming Sunday-school picnic in Mr. Harmon Andrews' field—right near the Lake of Shining Waters—particularly excited Anne?

   _____

   _____

   _____

2. What was the name Diana and Anne gave to their playhouse?

   _____

   _____

3. Mrs. Lynde says, "Blessed are they who expect nothing for they shall not be disappointed." But what did Anne think was the better way to enjoy life?

   _____

   _____

   _____

4. How had Marilla come to possess her amethyst brooch?

   _____

   _____

   _____

5. What was Marilla's punishment for Anne not confessing to stealing the brooch?

   _____

   _____

   _____

6. According to Anne's confession, how was the brooch lost?

   _____

   _____

   _____

7. What was Marilla's punishment for Anne losing the brooch?

_____

_____

_____

8. Where did Marilla end up finding the brooch?

_____

_____

_____

9. Recount the details of the *scrumptious* picnic.

_____

_____

_____

_____

_____

_____

ANNE OF GREEN GABLES
A Tempest in the School Teapot

1. Where was Lover's Lane?

   _____

   _____

2. Who was the school master dead gone on?

   _____

   _____

3. What was the first compliment Anne ever received?

   _____

   _____

   _____

4. Describe the handsome Gilbert Blythe.

   _____

   _____

   _____

   _____

5. What caused Anne to crack her slate on Gilbert's head?

   _____

   _____

   _____

6. Anne said "The iron has entered into my soul" and vowed to what?

   _____

   _____

   _____

7. What happened to Anne as a result of Mr. Phillips being seized with one of his spasmodic fits of reform?

_____

_____

_____

_____

8. What did Anne do with the little pink candy heart Gilbert gave to her?

_____

_____

_____

9. Mrs. Lynde dearly loved to be asked for advice. What advice did she give to Marilla when Anne vowed to never go back to school?

_____

_____

_____

10. What was Marilla's response to Anne's bitter woes over the future marriage of Diana far off in the future?

_____

_____

ANNE OF GREEN GABLES
Diana Is Invited to Tea with Tragic Results and *A New Interest in Life*

1. Why was Marilla going to be gone the day of the tragic tea?

   _____

   _____

   _____

2. What was Anne allowed to serve for the tea and on what?

   _____

   _____

   _____

   _____

3. What did Diana talk about with Anne while they shared apples?

   _____

   _____

   _____

4. What had been the unexpected result of Anne's pretending to be a nun taking the veil to bury a broken heart in cloistered seclusion?

   _____

   _____

   _____

5. Why did Diana insist on going home without any tea?

   _____

   _____

   _____

6. Why did Anne think prayer was a hopeless remedy to the misunderstanding that had come between her and Mrs. Barry?

_____

_____

_____

7. What gift did Diana give to Anne at their "eternal farewell?"

_____

_____

_____

8. Instead of dying of grief, Anne returned to school. What was given to her that showed her how much her imagination, singing and dramatic ability had been missed?

_____

_____

_____

_____

9. Describe the scholastic rivalry between Anne and Gilbert.

_____

_____

_____

_____

ANNE OF GREEN GABLES
Project—Raspberry Cordial

Supplies

2 pkg. frozen sweetened raspberries

1 1/4 c. sugar

3 lemons

4 c. boiling water

Directions

Put the unthawed raspberries into saucepan and add the sugar. Cook over medium heat, stirring once in a while, 20-25 minutes, until all the sugar has dissolved. With a potato masher mash the raspberries and syrup thoroughly. Pour the mixture through the strainer, making sure you extract all the juice. Discard the pulp. Squeeze 2 of the lemons and strain the juice. Add it to the raspberry juice. Boil 4 cups of water and add it to raspberry juice. Let raspberry cordial cool, and then chill it.

ANNE OF GREEN GABLES
Anne to the Rescue

1. What was the occasion to cause nearly all the men and a goodly proportion of the women of Avonlea to go to a town thirty miles away?

   _____

   _____

   _____

2. What way did Matthew vote, and what were the political leanings of Gilbert?"

   _____

   _____

3. What snack from the cellar was never eaten because of the unexpected arrival of Diana?

   _____

4. Why had Diana rushed over?

   _____

   _____

   _____

5. When Matthew left suddenly without a word, what course of action did Anne "read" in his thoughts?

   _____

   _____

   _____

6. What part did Mrs. Hammond play in keeping Anne so calm in the face of this emergency?

   _____

   _____

   _____

7. Describe Anne's treatment of Minnie May.

_____

_____

_____

8. Although the doctor did not tell Anne, what compliment did he pass along about Anne to the Barrys?

_____

_____

_____

9. What news did Marilla give to Anne after the blue plum preserves?

_____

_____

_____

10. What did Anne say that she felt was like heaping coals of fire on Mrs. Barry's head?

_____

_____

_____

11. In spite of her red hair, Anne felt perfectly happy that evening. What did such feelings inspire her to do?

_____

_____

_____

ANNE OF GREEN GABLES
Project—Taffy Pull

The Velvet Molasses Candy recipe below is taken from The Boston Cooking-School Cook Book *by Fannie Farmer, published by Little, Brown & Company, Boston, in 1896. It makes a delicious, buttery-tasting pull toffee. The Molasses Candy recipe is taken from the book* Practical Housewifery *by Marion Harland, published by Scribner, Armstrong & Co., New York, in 1874. Choose one of them to make to experience the vintage joys of a taffy pull.*

Velvet Molasses Candy

1 cup molasses

3 cups sugar

1 cup boiling water

3 tablespoons vinegar

1/2 teaspoon cream of tartar

1/2 cup melted butter

1/4 teaspoon soda

Put first four ingredients in kettle placed over front of range. As soon as boiling-point is reached, add cream of tartar. Boil until, when tried in cold water, mixture will become brittle. Stir constantly during last part of cooking. When nearly done, add butter and soda. Pour into a buttered pan and pull same as Molasses Candy. While pulling, add one teaspoon vanilla, one-half teaspoon lemon extract, few drops oil of peppermint, or few drops oil of wintergreen.

Molasses Candy

1 quart good molasses

1 cup vinegar

1 cup sugar

butter the size of an egg

1 teaspoonful baking soda

Dissolve the sugar in the vinegar, mix with the molasses, and boil, stirring frequently, until it hardens when dropped from the spoon into cold water; then stir in the butter and soda, the latter dissolved in hot water. Flavor to your taste, give one hard final stir, and pour into buttered dishes. As it cools, cut into squares for taffy, or, while soft enough to handle, pull white into sticks, using only the buttered tips of your fingers for that purpose.

ANNE OF GREEN GABLES
A Concert, a Catastrophe, and a Confession and *A Good Imagination Gone Wrong*

1. What news warranted five signal flashes of Diana's candle?

2. What argument convinced Marilla to change her mind about the big affair?

3. What was the only number on the program that failed to interest Anne?

4. What happened that caused Old Miss Barry to take back her promise to pay for a quarter's music lessons for Diana?

5. Why did Aunt Josephine consent to stay in Avonlea?

6. Who offered mayflowers to Anne in the Spring before the violets came into bloom?

7. What effect did headaches have on Marilla?

_____

_____

_____

8. What mistakes did Anne make on her Green Gables anniversary?

_____

_____

_____

_____

9. Describe the harrowing things that go on in the Haunted Wood.

_____

_____

_____

_____

_____

_____

_____

_____

ANNE OF GREEN GABLES
A New Departure in Flavorings and *Anne is Invited Out to Tea*

1. Why was it fortunate that Anne took an extra handkerchief to school?

   _____

   _____

2. Why were many a thing Mrs. Lynde had lent out returned that night, including quilting frames?

   _____

   _____

   _____

3. What aspects did Mrs. Lynde and Anne like about Mr. Allan?

   _____

   _____

   _____

4. What did Anne like about Mrs. Allan?

   _____

   _____

   _____

5. What was it about Mrs. Allan in contrast to Mr. Bell that made Anne want to be a Christian?

   _____

   _____

   _____

   _____

6. According to Anne, "tomorrow is a new day with no mistakes in it yet." What mistake did Anne make that Mrs. Allan found so funny?

_____

_____

_____

7. What about Mrs. Allan's invitation to Anne gave her such a thrill?

_____

_____

_____

8. While discussing Anne's visit to Mrs. Allan's, Marilla hit for once in her life on a very sound and pithy piece of advice? What was it?

_____

_____

_____

_____

_____

9. Anne thought she might like to be a minister's wife when she grew up. Why did she think that that was possible in spite of her red hair?

_____

_____

_____

_____

10. Summarize Anne's erroneous views on original sin.

_____

_____

_____

_____

_____

_____

11. What did Mrs. Lynde think was a "dangerous innovation"?

_____

_____

_____

ANNE OF GREEN GABLES
Project—Augustine for Anne

Anne may not have had a clear understanding of original sin, but as the wife of a Presbyterian minister, the author was well acquainted with the theological concept. *Read the following summary of this doctrine by St. Augustine from 415 A.D. and rewrite it in a simple (or unconventional) way that would have made sense to Anne.*

Human nature was certainly originally created blameless and without any fault; but the human nature by which each one of us is now born of Adam requires a physician, because it is not healthy. All good things, which it has by its conception, life, senses, and mind, it has from God, its creator and maker. But the weakness which disables these good natural qualities, as a result of which the nature needs enlightenment and healing, did not come from the blameless maker but from original sin, which was committed by free will. For this reason our guilty nature is liable to a just penalty. For if we are now a new creature in Christ, we were still children of wrath by nature, like everyone else. But God, who is rich in mercy, on account of the great love with which he loved us, even when we were dead through our sins, raised us up to life with Christ, by whose grace we are saved. But this grace of Christ, without which neither infants nor grown persons can be saved, is not bestowed as a reward for merits, but is given freely, which is why it is called *grace.*

_____

_____

_____

_____

_____

_____

_____

_____

ANNE OF GREEN GABLES

Anne Comes to Grief in an Affair of Honor
and *Miss Stacy and Her Pupils Get Up a Concert*

1. What did Josie Pye dare Anne to do?

   _____

   _____

   _____

2. What revelation did Marilla receive in the wake of Anne's accident?

   _____

   _____

   _____

3. How many times did Mrs. Allen visit Anne?

   _____

4. What did the new teacher instruct the children to do every morning and evening which Mrs. Lynde had never heard of a lady teacher doing?

   _____

   _____

5. Why could Anne say that she wrote the best compositions on their field afternoon nature studies without being guilty of vanity?

   _____

   _____

6. Anne was going to be in two dialogues—"The Society for the Suppression of Gossip" and "The Fairy Queen" for the Christmas concert. What was the laudable purpose for which the concert was being held?

   _____

   _____

ANNE OF GREEN GABLES
Matthew Insists on Puffed Sleeves
and *The Story Club Is Formed*

1. Matthew realized that there was something about Anne that was different from her mates, but was troubled by not being able to figure out what it was. Although it took two hours of smoking and hard reflection, Matthew arrived at a solution of his problem. What was the difference?

   The diffrence was that Anne was dreessed diffrently

2. What was almost as much a matter of conscience with the Cuthberts as attending the Presbyterian church and voting Conservative?

   Going to shop at william bliars was as much of a consience as voting conservative and going to preb chur

3. What did bangle bracelets make Matthew buy?

   bangle bracelets made him buy 20 Lbs of brown sugar and a rake.

4. What had Matthew looking so mysterious over and grinning about to himself?

   He was grinning and looking mysterious to himself because he made mrs rachel lynde make anne a puff sleeve dr

5. Breakfast seemed so commonplace Christmas morning. What did Anne prefer to feast on?

   She said she preffered to feast her eyes on the dress.

6. What did Aunt Josephine give to the Anne-girl for Christmas?

   Aunt Josephine gave Anne slippers for christmas.

7. What did Gilbert do at the concert that Diana thought was romantic?

   Gilbert was going on stage when Anne dropped a flower and gilbert put it in his chest pocket.

8. Why did Josie Pye and Julia Bell not "speak" for three months following the concert?

   They did not speack to each other because they gossiped, and mockeded each other after the concert.

9. What did Rosamond Montmorency insist upon?

   Rosamond Montmorency is

10. What effect did it have on Anne when Mrs. Allan told her that she was a dreadful mischief when she was a girl and was always getting into scrapes?

    It made her encouraged because she thought Mrs Allen was very good and she thought she was bad. So this inspired to try hardder.

ANNE OF GREEN GABLES
Vanity and Vexation of Spirit and *An Unfortunate Lily Maid*

1. For what did Anne think was worth being a little wicked?

   _____

   _____

2. What was the result of her "little" wickedness?

   _____

   _____

   _____

3. Marilla's headaches were getting worse and worse, but what did Marilla say that she was getting used to?

   _____

   _____

4. What did Diana tell Anne that made Anne flush sensitively with delight?

   _____

   _____

5. What was the name of the poet who wrote the poem that the girls were acting out?

   _____

   _____

6. What part did a sharp stake at the landing play in their performance?

   _____

   _____

   _____

7. Who saved Anne using Harmon Andrews' dory?

   _____

8. What did Anne's rescuer ask once they reached the shore?

_____

_____

_____

9. Fill in what Anne was "cured of" through the following mistakes:

The Amethyst Brooch Affair: _____

The Haunted Wood: _____

The Liniment Cake: _____

The German Jew Dyeing: _____

Sinking of the Barry Flat: _____

10. What did Matthew encourage Anne not to give up?

_____

_____

_____

_____

ANNE OF GREEN GABLES
Project 1—Elaine of Astolat in Art

Elaine the White, or sometimes called Elaine the Fair, is a famous figure in Arthurian legend who dies of her unrequited love for Lancelot. Although the daughter of Bernard of Astolat fails to capture Lancelot's heart, she has caught the imaginations of many artists over the years. *Research the following artists and identify who you think did the best job depicting the Lady of Shalott.*

Dante Gabriel Rossetti

William Holman Hunt

John William Waterhouse

Howard Pyle

Louis Rhead

Elizabeth Siddal

ANNE OF GREEN GABLES
Project 2—Tennyson's The Lady of Shalott

Anne would think that you were ever so romantic if you read this famous poem.
Perhaps you might even memorize a portion of it.

Part I.

On either side the river lie
Long fields of barley and of rye,
That clothe the wold and meet the sky;
And thro' the field the road runs by
    To many-tower'd Camelot;
And up and down the people go,
Gazing where the lilies blow
Round an island there below,
    The island of Shalott.

Willows whiten, aspens quiver,
Little breezes dusk and shiver
Thro' the wave that runs for ever
By the island in the river
    Flowing down to Camelot.
Four gray walls, and four gray towers,
Overlook a space of flowers,
And the silent isle imbowers
    The Lady of Shalott.

By the margin, willow-veil'd
Slide the heavy barges trail'd
By slow horses; and unhail'd
The shallop flitteth silken-sail'd
    Skimming down to Camelot:
But who hath seen her wave her hand?
Or at the casement seen her stand?
Or is she known in all the land,
    The Lady of Shalott?

Only reapers, reaping early
In among the bearded barley,
Hear a song that echoes cheerly
From the river winding clearly,
    Down to tower'd Camelot:
And by the moon the reaper weary,
Piling sheaves in uplands airy,
Listening, whispers "Tis the fairy
    Lady of Shalott."

Part II.

There she weaves by night and day
A magic web with colours gay.
She has heard a whisper say,
A curse is on her if she stay
    To look down to Camelot.
She knows not what the curse may be,
And so she weaveth steadily,
And little other care hath she,
    The Lady of Shalott.

And moving thro' a mirror clear
That hangs before her all the year,
Shadows of the world appear.
There she sees the highway near
    Winding down to Camelot:
There the river eddy whirls,
And there the surly village-churls,
And the red cloaks of market girls,
    Pass onward from Shalott.

Sometimes a troop of damsels glad,
An abbot on an ambling pad,
Sometimes a curly shepherd-lad,
Or long-hair'd page in crimson clad,
    Goes by to tower'd Camelot;
And sometimes thro' the mirror blue
The knights come riding two and two:
She hath no loyal knight and true,
    The Lady of Shalott.

But in her web she still delights
To weave the mirror's magic sights,
For often thro' the silent nights
A funeral, with plumes and lights
    And music, went to Camelot:
Or when the moon was overhead,
Came two young lovers lately wed;
"I am half-sick of shadows," said
    The Lady of Shalott.

ANNE OF GREEN GABLES
Project 2, Page 2

Part III.
A bow-shot from her bower-eaves,
He rode between the barley-sheaves,
The sun came dazzling thro' the leaves,
And flamed upon the brazen greaves
    Of bold Sir Lancelot.
A redcross knight for ever kneel'd
To a lady in his shield,
That sparkled on the yellow field,
    Beside remote Shalott.

The gemmy bridle glitter'd free,
Like to some branch of stars we see
Hung in the golden Galaxy.
The bridle-bells rang merrily
    As he rode down to Camelot:
And from his blazon'd baldric slung
A mighty silver bugle hung,
And as he rode his armour rung,
    Beside remote Shalott.

All in the blue unclouded weather
Thick-jewell'd shone the saddle-leather,
The helmet and the helmet-feather
Burn'd like one burning flame together,
    As he rode down to Camelot.
As often thro' the purple night,
Below the starry clusters bright,
Some bearded meteor, trailing light,
    Moves over still Shalott.

His broad clear brow in sunlight glow'd;
On burnish'd hooves his war-horse trode;
From underneath his helmet flow'd
His coal-black curls as on he rode,
    As he rode down to Camelot.
From the bank and from the river
He flash'd into the crystal mirror,
"Tirra lirra," by the river
    Sang Sir Lancelot.

She left the web, she left the loom,
She made three paces thro' the room,
She saw the water-lily bloom,
She saw the helmet and the plume,
    She look'd down to Camelot.
Out flew the web and floated wide;
The mirror crack'd from side to side;
"The curse is come upon me," cried
    The Lady of Shalott.

     Part IV.
In the stormy east-wind straining,
The pale-yellow woods were waning,
The broad stream in his banks complaining,
Heavily the low sky raining
    Over tower'd Camelot;
Down she came and found a boat
Beneath a willow left afloat,
And round about the prow she wrote
    The Lady of Shalott.

And down the river's dim expanse--
Like some bold seër in a trance,
Seeing all his own mischance--
With a glassy countenance
    Did she look to Camelot.
And at the closing of the day
She loosed the chain, and down she lay;
The broad stream bore her far away,
    The Lady of Shalott.

Lying, robed in snowy white
That loosely flew to left and right--
The leaves upon her falling light--
Thro' the noises of the night
    She floated down to Camelot:
And as the boat-head wound along
The willowy hills and fields among,
They heard her singing her last song,
    The Lady of Shalott.

Heard a carol, mournful, holy,
Chanted loudly, chanted lowly,
Till her blood was frozen slowly,
And her eyes were darken'd wholly,
    Turn'd to tower'd Camelot;
For ere she reach'd upon the tide
The first house by the water-side,
Singing in her song she died,
    The Lady of Shalott.

Under tower and balcony,
By garden-wall and gallery,
A gleaming shape she floated by,
A corse between the houses high,
    Silent into Camelot.
Out upon the wharfs they came,
Knight and burgher, lord and dame,
And round the prow they read her name,
    The Lady of Shalott.

Who is this? and what is here?
And in the lighted palace near
Died the sound of royal cheer;
And they cross'd themselves for fear,
    All the knights at Camelot:
But Lancelot mused a little space;
He said, "She has a lovely face;
God in his mercy lend her grace,
    The Lady of Shalott."

ANNE OF GREEN GABLES
An Epoch in Anne's Life and *The Queens Class Is Organized*

1. Why isn't Charlotte Gillis going to be married in the church?

   _____

   _____

   _____

   _____

2. What was the news that Diana gave Anne on that purple dream evening?

   _____

   _____

   _____

   _____

3. Why was Marilla now making only fashionable dresses for Anne?

   _____

   _____

   _____

   _____

4. Avonlea was pretty well represented at the Exhibition with Josie Pye, Mr. Andrews, Mr. Bell, and Clara Louise MacPherson all getting prizes for their submissions. For what was Mrs. Lynde awarded first prize?

   _____

   _____

   _____

5. What did Anne decide was as good as having an extra conscience?

_____

_____

6. What was instrumental in helping Anne to return to common life again after Madame Selitsky's performance?

_____

_____

7. Although Anne enjoyed every minute of her time with Miss Barry and even hugged and kissed her at their parting, what about the old woman did Anne not like?

_____

_____

8. What was "the best of it all" about Anne's trip to town to visit Aunt Josephine?

_____

_____

9. Why did Marilla perform a sort of unconscious penance by being strict and critical of Anne?

_____

_____

10. Miss Stacy took all the girls in their teens down to the brook Wednesday to discuss solemn things. What did she tell the girls?

_____

_____

_____

11. What did Miss Stacy catch Anne doing when she should have been studying Canadian history?

_____

_____

_____

12. What has been the dream of Anne's life--that is, for the last six months?

_____

_____

_____

13. Why did Jane Andrews decide to devote her whole life to teaching, and never, never marry?

_____

_____

_____

_____

14. What did Anne shroud "in deepest oblivion?"

_____

_____

_____

15. What was the reason Marilla missed the Aid meeting at the end of the chapter?

_____

_____

_____

_____

ANNE OF GREEN GABLES
Project 1—The Gray Fairy

"All the little wood things—the ferns and the satin leaves and the crackerberries—have gone to sleep, just as if somebody had tucked them away until spring under a blanket of leaves." *Draw the little gray fairy with a rainbow scarf that came tiptoeing along in the moonlight night who Anne imagined doing it.*

ANNE OF GREEN GABLES
Project 2—The Preacher(s)

"Moody Spurgeon is going to be a minister. Mrs. Lynde says he couldn't be anything else with a name like that to live up to. I hope it isn't wicked of me, Marilla, but really the thought of Moody Spurgeon being a minister makes me laugh. He's such a funny-looking boy with that big fat face, and his little blue eyes, and his ears sticking out like flaps. But perhaps he will be more intellectual looking when he grows up." *Research Dwight Lyman Moody or Charles Haddon Spurgeon and write a paragraph about that man's ministry.*

ANNE OF GREEN GABLES
Where the Brook and River Meet and *The Pass List Is Out*

1. Why did Marilla offer no objections to Anne's gypsyings that summer?

_____

_____

_____

2. Who makes Marilla and Anne feel really bad and unregenerate, and why?

3. What impact did flounces have on Anne?

4. Marilla noticed that Anne didn't chatter half as much as she used to, nor use half as many big words. What was Anne's reason for this change?

5. According to Mrs. Lynde, what should you do if you can't be cheerful?

6. What was Moody Spurgeon muttering to himself to steady his nerves?

    _____

    _____

7. What did Anne mean when she told Diana that she'd rather not pass at all than not come out pretty well up on the list?

    _____

    _____

    _____

8. How did Ned and Jimmy both win and lose their bets?

    _____

    _____

    _____

9. What did Mrs. Lynde say (and far be it from her to be backward in saying it) to the news of the Pass List?

    _____

    _____

    _____

    _____

ANNE OF GREEN GABLES
The Hotel Concert and *A Queen's Girl*

1. How had Anne's room changed since she took residence there four years earlier?

   _____

   _____

   _____

   _____

   _____

2. Why did Diana call Anne an elocutionist?

   _____

   _____

3. Diana was beginning to have a reputation in Avonlea for notable taste in dressing, but to what had she sadly resigned herself?

   _____

   _____

4. What shook Anne free from her attack of stage fright?

   _____

   _____

   _____

5. What compliment did the distinguished artist from America bestow upon Anne?

   _____

   _____

6. If it wasn't the recitation of "The Maiden's Vow" that made Marilla cry, what was it?

_____

_____

_____

7. Who was the only person in Anne's class at Queens who she knew?

_____

8. Why didn't Anne board with Miss Josephine Barry?

_____

_____

_____

9. Why did Josie come by to visit Anne?

_____

_____

_____

10. What ambition did Anne add to her goal of achieving First Class, at the end of the year, and perhaps the medal?

_____

_____

_____

ANNE OF GREEN GABLES
The Winter at Queen's and *The Glory and the Dream*

1. Although she didn't understand half the things Gilbert Blythe said, describe the person Gilbert chose to walk home with from the Carmody station every Friday night.

   _____

   _____

   _____

   _____

2. Who were the two girls at the Academy who formed Anne's little circle of friends?

   _____

   _____

   _____

3. Anne spent many of her spare hours at Beechwood and generally ate her Sunday dinners there and went to church with Miss Barry. While there, what did Anne do for Miss Barry which saved the woman a great deal of trouble?

   _____

   _____

   _____

   _____

4. What did Anne think made exams seem rather unimportant?

   _____

   _____

5. Why did the students cheer for Anne at the end of the term?

   _____

   _____

6. Why wasn't Anne's "friend the enemy" attending Redmond in September along with Anne?

   _____

   _____

7. Describe the condition of the Cuthberts' health.

    _____

    _____

    _____

8. What financial news had Rachel shared with Marilla?

    _____

    _____

9. What was Matthew's response to Anne's regret of not being a boy in order to help more around the farm?

    _____

    _____

    _____

ANNE OF GREEN GABLES
The Reaper Whose Name Is Death and *The Bend in the Road*

1. What was the shock which caused Matthew's death?

   _____

   _____

2. In the wake of Marilla's impassioned grief after her brother's death, what did Diana find hard to understand?

   _____

   _____

3. What was Marilla able to confess to Anne while Anne mourned?

   _____

   _____

   _____

4. What did Anne tell Mrs. Allan seemed to her like a disloyalty to Matthew?

   _____

   _____

   _____

5. What "bit of romance" had Marilla once had in her life and what had put the end to it?

   _____

   _____

   _____

6. What did the oculist instruct Marilla?

   _____

   _____

   _____

7. What did Anne look courageously in the face and found it a friend?

   _____

8. What plan did Anne devise to keep Green Gables from being sold?

_____

_____

_____

9. Besides sharing that it's a great blessing not to be fat and predicting that Anne would kill herself studying Greek and Latin, what useful information did Mrs. Lynde share about Gilbert Blythe?

_____

_____

_____

_____

10. What "complete confession" did Anne make the following evening?

_____

_____

_____

11. What did Marilla ask Anne which made her blush?

_____

_____

12. What was Anne's reaction to reflection on the joy of sincere work, worthy aspiration, congenial friendship and the bend in the road?

_____

_____

ANNE OF GREEN GABLES
Project—The Book vs. the Movie

Anne of Green Gables is a 1985 television movie based on the novels *Anne of Green Gables* **and** *Anne of Avonlea* (so you should read *Anne of Avonlea* before watching the film). Lucy Maud Montgomery's famous books have inspired sequels, prequels, spin-offs and even Japanese anime, but this version is by far the best. In fact, most other film adaptations should be avoided. This critically-acclaimed motion picture stars Megan Follows, Tony Award-winner Colleen Dewhurst, and Academy Award-nominee Richard Farnsworth. The film first aired on December 1, 1985, and has now been translated and seen in more places around the world than the original novels.

Watch the movie and take note of what occurs in the movie that is different from what happened in the book. Then write a short defense of your favorite element of the movie that was different from the book.

_____

_____

_____

_____

_____

_____

_____

_____

I prefer in the movie how . . .

_____

_____

_____

ANNE OF GREEN GABLES
Who's Who Appendix

Unless you're Rachel Lynde, you may have trouble keeping all the names in this story straight. Following is a brief overview of some of the characters in Anne of Green Gables.

Mr. Abbey was the owner of Abbey Bank. "Matthew said any bank with him at the head of it was good enough for anybody."

Mr. Allan was a minister for Avonlea. Anne "liked him because his sermon was interesting and he prayed as if he meant it and not just as if he did it because he was in the habit of it."

Mrs. Allan "has a lovely smile; she has such exquisite dimples in her cheeks" and is the wife of the minister. When she was a little girl she was "always getting into scrapes".

Alice Andrews was a girl from Anne's Avonlea class who was going to bring a new Pansy book to Anne.

Billy Andrews was Jane Andrew's brother. He drove Anne and Jane to the White Sands Hotel for a concert. "He was a big, fat, stolid youth of twenty, with a round, expressionless face, and a painful lack of conversational gifts."

Harmon Andrews was the host to a Sunday-school picnic, a Grit, and "a perfect old crank, . . . meaner than second skimmings."

Jane Andrews was a girl in Anne's circle of friends, a member of the Story Club, and a part of the prep class for Queen's.

Malcolm Andrews was a young man who proposed to Susan Gillis by telling her that he had been given the farm by his dad.

Minnie Andrews was a model pupil of Mr. Phillips's who Anne had to once sit with in school.

Prissy Andrews was an older student studying for the entrance examination into Queen's Academy at Charlottetown with Mr. Phillips, the schoolmaster who was "dead gone" on her.

Timothy Andrews swept the school and kindled the fire.

Diana Barry was Anne's soulfriend, neighbor, and friend who "always laughed before she spoke."

Minnie May Barry was Diana's sister who got croup.

Mr. Barry was Diana's father.

Mrs. Barry was Diana's strict mother, "a woman of strong prejudices and dislikes, and her anger was of the cold, sullen sort which is always hardest to overcome."

Josephine Barry was Diana's rich, "thin, prim and rigid" great-aunt.

Julia Bell was a freckled girl whose name was written with Gilbert Blythe's on the school porch wall under a "Take Notice" sign. Her sister Alice has "a crooked nose," and her father Andrew's woods overshadow the Violet Vale.

Mr. Bell was the Sunday School superintendent. His wife made ice cream with Rachel Lynde for the picnic at Harmon Andrews' field.

Robert Bell and his family lived up the road from Mrs. Rachel Lynde and their farm was located on the west side of the Cuthbert's property.

Mr. Bentley was Avonlea's minister for 18 years. He resigned one year after Anne came to town.

William J. Blair owned a store in Carmody. His wife Winnie Adella sang at a benefit concert at the White Sands hotel.

Mrs. Peter Blewett was a "small, shrewish faced woman without an ounce of superflouous flesh on her bones" who was interested in adopting Anne to care for her large family.

Gilbert Blythe was an "aw'fly handsome" boy with "curly brown hair, roguish hazel eyes and a mouth twisted into a teasing smile." He and Anne did not always share a cordial relationship.

ANNE OF GREEN GABLES
Who's Who Appendix

John Blythe was Gilbert's father, and he and Marilla were once really good friends.

Katie Boulter was an aquaintance of Anne's who "gave her a perfume bottle to keep slate-water in." Her sister Tillie let Anne "wear her bead ring" the first day of school, and her brother Sam "sassed" Mr. Phillips" in class and Mr. Phillips whipped him.

Lauretta Bradley was a very nice little girl. "Not exactly a kindred spirit, you know, but still very nice."

Jerry Buote was a boy hired by Matthew who said that Anne "talked all the time to herself or to the trees and flowers like a crazy girl."

Aurelia Clay was the girl who Anthony Pye "poured the last drops of water from his slate bottle" down the back of her neck.

Marilla Cuthbert was "a tall, thin woman, with angles and without curves; her dark hair showed some gray streaks and was always twisted up in a hard knot behind with two wire hairpins stuck aggressively through it." She and her brother adopted Anne.

Matthew Cuthbert was Marilla's brother. Together they owned Green Gables. He was also a Conservative.

Rosalia DeVere was the name Anne imagined Hepzibah Jenkins having.

Cordelia Fitzgerald was Anne as she once imagined herself—"tall and regal, clad in a gown of trailing white lace, with a pearl cross on my breast and pearls in my hair."

Ruby Gillis was one of the many Gillis girls. Ruby was inclined toward sentimentality and hysterical fits. She cared more for her good looks and her string of boyfriends than she did for her studies. Her sister Jenny's figure matched Anne's so much that when Mrs. Lynde made a dress for Anne, she used Jenny as the model. Ruby also had a brother named Jack, a sister named Charlotte (who won't be getting married in a church), another sister named Emily (who Marilla commented "has got taste"), and sisters Sara and Susan.

Jimmy Glover was a school mate who lost a bet with Ned Wright.

Mrs. Hammond was a woman who found Anne handy with children and took care of her for over two years up the river from Marysville until Mr. Hammond died. She had eight children of which six were twins three times.

Lucilla Harris was the niece of Samuel Lawson's wife who worked in his store and wore "several bangle bracelets that glittered and rattled and tinkled with every movement of her hands."

Hepzibah Jenkins was a girl that Anne knew at the orphan asylum. Hepzibah was also the name of the mother of Manasseh, king of Judah in 2 Kings 21:1. Her name means "my delight is in her."

Samuel Lawson was a store owner in Carmody.

Rachel Lynde "lived just where the Avonlea main road dipped down into a little hollow, fringed with alders and ladies' eardrops and traversed by a brook." She was a notable housewife; her work was always done and well done; she "ran" the Sewing Circle, helped run the Sunday-school, and was the strongest prop of the Church Aid Society and Foreign Missions Auxiliary.

Thomas Lynde was "Rachel Lynde's husband"

Moody Spurgeon MacPherson was a classmate of Anne's in Avonlea and at Queens. He had a "big fat face . . little blue eyes, and his ears [stuck] out like flaps." Ella May and Minnie were his sisters.

Katie Maurice was one of Anne's imaginary friends in the bookcase mirror while Anne lived with Mr. and Mrs. Thomas.

Stella Maynard was a friend of Anne's at Queen's who "had a heartful of wistful dreams and fancies, as aerial and rainbow-like as Anne's own."

Rosamond Montmorency was the alias that Anne used in the story club that she founded.

ANNE OF GREEN GABLES
Who's Who Appendix

Josie Pye was nemisis of Anne's in Avonlea and at Queen's.

Miss Rogerson was Anne's Sunday-school teacher who asked Anne a lot of questions on Anne's first day of Sunday-school.

Geraldine Seymour was one of Anne's fictional characters in "The Jealous Rival"; also, called "Death Not Divided."

Bertha Shirley was the mother of Anne Shirley who was a teacher at Bolingbroke High School until she married Walter Shirley. She died three months of the fever after Anne was born. Walter died four days later.

Charlie Sloane was a boy at the Avonlea school who was "dead gone" on Anne. His sister's name was Carrie.

Mrs. Alexander Spencer arranged the adoption for Matthew and Marilla Cuthbert.

Robert Spencer was Mrs. Spencer's brother who was asked by Matthew and Marilla to tell Mrs. Spencer to adopt a boy.

Muriel Stacy was the first woman teacher of Avonlea. According to Diana Barry, "she has the loveliest fair curly hair and such fascinating eyes." Anne found that "Miss Stacy was a bright, sympathetic young woman with the happy gift of winning and holding the affections of her pupils and bringing out the best that was in them mentally and morally."

Mrs. Thomas took Anne in when her parents died of the fever. She was poor. Her husband was a drunk. He died falling under a train when Anne was eight years old.

Violetta was Anne's imaginary friend while she stayed with Mr. and Mrs. Hammond who would echo Anne's words back in the green valley near the Hammond's house.

Lewis Wilson was one of the three serious gold medal contestants at Queen's.

Ned Wright lost a bet with Jimmy Glover

ANNE OF GREEN GABLES
Answers

CHAPTERS 1
1. by the time it reached Lynde's Hollow it was a quiet, well-conducted little stream
2. she had knitted sixteen "cotton warp" quilts
3. where Matthew Cuthbert was going and why was he going there
4. it would have been cheerful if it had not been so painfully clean as to give it something of the appearance of an unused parlor
5. Marilla was a tall, thin woman, with angles and without curves; her dark hair showed some gray streaks and was always twisted up in a hard little knot behind with two wire hairpins stuck aggressively through it. She looked like a woman of narrow experience and rigid conscience, which she was; but there was a saving something about her mouth which, if it had been ever so slightly developed, might have been considered indicative of a sense of humor.
6. Matthew had gone to Bright River to get a little boy from an orphan asylum in Nova Scotia.
7. Adopting a child was a mighty foolish thing because you don't know a single thing about him nor what his disposition is like nor what sort of parents he had nor how he's likely to turn out. Not only that, but Rachel read how a man and his wife took a boy out of an orphan asylum and he set fire to the house at night, and another case where an adopted boy used to suck the eggs.

CHAPTER 2
1. Marilla and Mrs. Rachel
2. . . . he was an odd-looking personage, with an ungainly figure and long iron-gray hair that touched his stooping shoulders, and a full, soft brown beard which he had worn ever since he was twenty.
3. walking up to a girl—a strange girl—an orphan girl—and demand of her why she wasn't a boy.
4. A child of about eleven, garbed in a very short, very tight, very ugly dress of yellowish-gray wincey. She wore a faded brown sailor hat and beneath the hat, extending down her back, were two braids of very thick, decidedly red hair. Her face was small, white and thin, also much freckled; her mouth was large and so were her eyes, which looked green in some lights and moods and gray in others. Her chin was very pointed and pronounced, her forehead was

broad and full. *Lucy Maud Montgomery used a photograph of Evelyn Nesbit—clipped from an American magazine and pasted to the wall next to her writing desk—as the model for the heroine of this book. Nesbit was also the subject of the famous Charles Dana Gibson drawing entitled "Women: the Eternal Question," published in 1905. Sculptor George Grey Barnard used her for his famous study "Innocence," which is in the collection of the Metropolitan Museum of Art. Nesbit was noted for her entanglement in the murder of her ex-lover, architect Stanford White, by her first husband, Harry Kendall Thaw. She died in a nursing home in Santa Monica, California on January 17, 1967, at the age of 82.*

5. "I had made up my mind that if you didn't come for me to-night I'd go down the track to that big wild cherry-tree at the bend, and climb up into it to stay all night. "
6. wicked
7. a foreign missionary
8. her hair color
9. the Avenue/the White Way of Delight
10. Barry's Pond

ANNE OF GREEN GABLES
Answers

CHAPTERS 3-4
1. he had never even asked her name
2. that was the name Anne wanted to be called
3. If it was spelled with an E. *The author preferred to be called Maud—without an E, and was annoyed when people spelled it incorrectly.*
4. She was in the depths of despair.
5. Anne's room consisted of bare whitewashed walls, a round braided mat in the middle of the floor, a high, old-fashioned bed, with four dark, low-turned posts, a three-corner table adorned with a fat, red velvet pin-cushion, a little six-by-eight mirror, and a window with an icy white muslin frill over it. *Green Gables, located in Cavendish in the Prince Edward Island National Park, is a popular tourist destination. You can get a virtual tour of Anne's room (and the rest of the house) at www.gov.pe.ca/greengables.*
6. Matthew was smoking—he seldom smoked, but at certain times and seasons he felt driven to it.
7. She forgot to turn back the bedclothes.
8. hold her tongue
9. Bonny

CHAPTERS 5-6
1. Anne was born in Bolingbroke, Nova Scotia a little over eleven years earlier to poor teachers who both died of a fever after Anne was born. She lived with the Thomas family until she was eight, and then lived with the Hammonds to help with their eight children. After two years she was sent to the asylum at Hopeton. Four months later Mrs. Spencer took her to Avonlea.
2. Mrs. Peter Blewett needed a girl to help care for her family of pert, quarrelsome children.
3. instead of wanting to return Anne that very day, Marilla said that she had just come over to find out how the mistake had occurred.
4. Marilla insisted that she would raise the child and that Matthew would not interfere with her methods.
5. Matthew agreed but added, "Only be as good and kind to her as you can without spoiling her."

CHAPTERS 7-8
1. infinite, eternal and unchangeable; goodness, truth *Westminster Shorter Catechism (1674)—Question 4: What is God? Answer: God is a Spirit, infinite, eternal, and unchangeable, in his being, wisdom, power, holiness, justice, goodness, and truth.*
2. splendid words that sounded like a big organ playing
3. because Mrs. Thomas told Anne that God made her hair red on purpose
4. thank God for your blessings and ask Him humbly for the things you want *The prayer Marilla intended to teach Anne was from a classic children's prayer from the 18th century. The version printed in* The New England Primer *goes: Now I lay me down to sleep, I pray the Lord my soul to keep; Should I die before I wake, I pray the Lord my soul to take.*
5. stay at Green Gables; to be good-looking when she grew up/"I remain, Yours respectfully, Anne Shirley."
6. she cried
7. Aunt Marilla
8. She talked about her prayers.
9. Anne thought the artist shouldn't have painted Jesus looking so sorrowful.
10. a bosom friend—an intimate friend
11. Marilla was as fond of morals and was firmly convinced that one should be tacked on to every remark made to a child who was being brought up.
12. her friend in the bookcase of Mrs. Thomas

CHAPTERS 9-10
1. Marilla permitted the "chatter" until she found herself becoming too interested in the stories.
2. Rachel had called her skinny, ugly, freckled and red-headed.
3. She insisted that Anne apologize.
4. "because, whenever she recalled Mrs. Rachel's dumbfounded countenance, her lips twitched with amusement and she felt a most reprehensible desire to laugh."
5. since the spring he helped Marilla paper the spare bedroom, four years before
6. Mrs. Lynde offered her the hope that Anne's hair might darken to a real handsome auburn.
7. because she was homely
8. Anne suddenly came close to Marilla and slipped her hand into the older woman's hard palm.
9. "Saying one's prayers isn't exactly the same thing as praying."

ANNE OF GREEN GABLES
Answers

CHAPTERS 11–12

1. to avoid pampering Anne's vanity
2. warnings of a sick headache
3. They looked at her and whispered to each other behind their quarterlies. Nobody made any friendly advances.
4. Seeing a long row of white birches hanging over the lake and the sunshine fell down through them, Anne prayed, "Thank you for it, God," two or three times.
5. because Anne's comments were what she herself had really thought deep down in her heart for years, but had never given expression to.
6. Lots of little girls there had bouquets pinned on their dresses and lots of the little girls had artificial flowers on their hats.
7. Marilla said, "It's her mother you've got to reckon with. If she doesn't like you it won't matter how much Diana does."
8. perhaps Anne would take her more out-of-doors
9. They imagined the path was running water.
10. a perfectly beautiful picture of a lovely lady in a pale blue silk dress/half of her chocolate sweeties

CHAPTERS 13–14

1. ice cream
2. Idlewild
3. Anne believed that looking forward to things was half the pleasure of them. "You mayn't get the things themselves; but nothing can prevent you from having the fun of looking forward to them."
4. A seafaring uncle had given it to her mother who in turn had bequeathed it to Marilla.
5. Anne was not allowed to go anywhere—even the church picnic—until she had confessed.
6. Anne took the amethyst brooch and pinned it on her breast. Then going over the bridge across the Lake of Shining Waters she took the brooch off to have another look at it, and dropped it. ". . . it just slipped through my fingers—so—and went down—down—down, all purplysparkling, and sank forevermore beneath the Lake of Shining Waters."
7. Anne was not allowed to go to the church picnic.
8. hanging to a thread of the lace of Marilla's best black shawl
9. a splendid tea, a row on the Lake of Shining Waters (Jane Andrews nearly fell overboard), and ice cream

CHAPTER 15

1. Lover's Lane opened out below the orchard at Green Gables and stretched far up into the woods to the end of the Cuthbert farm. It was the way by which the cows were taken to the back pasture and the wood hauled home in winter.
2. Prissy Andrews
3. Jane Andrews told Anne that Minnie MacPherson told her that she heard Prissy Andrews tell Sara Gillis that Anne had a very pretty nose.
4. He was a tall boy, with curly brown hair, roguish hazel eyes, and a mouth twisted into a teasing smile.
5. Gilbert teased her—he called her "carrots."
6. Anne vowed to never forgive Gilbert Blythe.
7. Anne had to sit with Gilbert Blythe.
8. Anne arose, took the pink heart gingerly between the tips of her fingers, dropped it on the floor, ground it to powder beneath her heel, and resumed her position without deigning to bestow a glance on Gilbert.
9. Rachel said she'd humor Anne a little at first, let her stay home, and not mention school to Anne again until she said it herself.
10. Marilla collapsed on the nearest chair and burst into such a hearty and unusual peal of laughter that Matthew, crossing the yard outside, halted in amazement.

CHAPTERS 16–17

1. She was attending a meeting of the Aid Society at Carmody.
2. She was allowed to use the old brown tea set, open the little yellow crock of cherry preserves, cut some fruit cake and have some of the cookies and snaps. Also there was a bottle half full of raspberry cordial that was left over from the church social that they could have—and a cooky to eat with it.
3. school gossip
4. Anne forgot all about covering the pudding sauce and the next morning she found a mouse drowned in that pudding sauce!
5. Diana felt "awful dizzy" and was, in fact, drunk.
6. According to Anne, not even "God Himself can do very much with such an obstinate person as Mrs. Barry."
7. In addition to her declaration of love for Anne, Diana consented to give her a lock of her "jet-black tresses."
8. three blue plums, an enormous yellow pansy cut from the covers of a floral catalogue, a perfectly

elegant new pattern of knit lace, a perfume bottle to keep slate-water in, a piece of pale pink paper decorated with poetry, a big luscious "strawberry apple." a slate pencil, gorgeously bedizened with striped red and yellow paper (costing two cents where ordinary pencils cost only one), and finally —a new book-marker out of red tissue paper from Diana Barry

9. The rivalry was entirely good natured on Gilbert's side, but the same thing cannot be said of Anne. In the end, Gilbert beat her because of Algebra (there is no scope for imagination in it at all).

CHAPTER 18

1. the decision of a certain Canadian Premier to include Prince Edward Island in a political tour
2. Conservative; the boys in school were Grits *(nickname of the Liberal party from 1884 on)*
3. russets—winter apples that Matthew never ate
4. Minnie May was awful sick—she had the croup.
5. that he was going to harness the sorrel mare to go to Carmody for the doctor
6. Anne knew exactly what to do for croup because Mrs. Hammond had twins three times, and when you look after three pairs of twins you naturally get a lot of experience.
7. Anne scolded Mary Joe into heating water, undressed Minnie May and put her to bed in some soft flannel cloths. Then she administered dose after dose of ipecac until every drop of ipecac was gone. *Interestingly, doctors nowadays strongly advise against the use of this syrup! The artwork on this page is an illustration of the ipecac plant.*
8. Anne "is as smart as they make 'em. I tell you she saved that baby's life, for it would have been too late by the time I got there. She seems to have a skill and presence of mind perfectly wonderful in a child of her age."
9. Mrs. Barry had visited, and said that she was very sorry she acted as she did in that affair of the currant wine, and that she hoped Anne would forgive her and that Anne would be good friends with Diana again.
10. "I have no hard feelings for you, Mrs. Barry. I assure you once for all that I did not mean to intoxicate Diana and henceforth I shall cover the past with the mantle of oblivion."
11. Anne felt like praying—and even thinking out a special brand-new prayer in honor of the occasion.

CHAPTERS 19-20

1. an invitation for a sleep-over and a concert—and sleeping in the spare bedroom
2. "I think you ought to let Anne go," repeated over and over
3. "Bingen on the Rhine" recited by Gilbert Blythe, especially when he came to the line, "There's another, not a sister," and looked right down at Anne.
4. jumping on Aunt Josephine in the middle of the night
5. "for the sake of getting better acquainted with that Anne-girl"
6. It was the person whose name Anne vowed never to let cross her lips. (Gilbert)
7. Headaches always left Marilla somewhat sarcastic.
8. She starched Matthew's handkerchiefs and burned the pie to a crisp.
9. There's a white lady walks along the brook just about this time of the night and wrings her hands and utters wailing cries. She appears when there is to be a death in the family. And the ghost of a little murdered child haunts the corner up by Idlewild; it creeps up behind you and lays its cold fingers on your hand. And there's a headless man stalks up and down the path and skeletons glower at you between the boughs.

CHAPTERS 21-22

1. Mr. Phillips's departure made all the girls cry.
2. A new minister, and moreover a minister with a wife, was a lawful object of curiosity in a quiet little country settlement so everyone was visiting with whatever excuse they could find, including Marilla returning the quilting frames.
3. Anne liked him because his sermon was interesting and he prayed as if he meant it and not just as if he did it because he was in the habit of it. Mrs. Lynde liked him because his theology was sound and because his wife's people were most respectable and the women were all good housekeepers. Mrs. Lynde says ". . . sound doctrine in the man and good housekeeping in the woman make an ideal combination for a minister's family."
4. Mrs. Allan said she didn't think it was fair for the teacher to ask all the questions. She said that Anne and her classmates could ask her any question they liked.
5. Mrs. Allan introduced Anne to the idea that religion could be a cheerful thing. Mr. Bell had made her

ANNE OF GREEN GABLES
Answers

think that Chrisitianity was kind of melancholy. Mr. Superintendent Bell was a good person but he didn't seem to get any comfort out of it. In contrast, Anne could tell that Mrs. Allan was glad she was a Christian and that she'd be one even if she could get to heaven without it.

6. Anne flavored that cake with Anodyne Liniment.
7. Mrs. Allan wrote 'Miss Anne Shirley, Green Gables' on the letter ant that was the first time Anne was ever called 'Miss.'
8. Marilla said, "The trouble with you, Anne, is that you're thinking too much about yourself. You should just think of Mrs. Allan and what would be nicest and most agreeable to her."
9. A minister mightn't mind my red hair because he wouldn't be thinking of such worldly things.
10. Anne believed that some people are naturally good and others are not. Anne was one of "the others." Mrs. Lynde told the red-haired girl that Anne was full of original sin. No matter how hard she tried to be good, Anne could never make such a success of it as those who are "naturally good."
11. a female teacher in Avonlea

Project—Augustine for Anne
Answers will vary. One possible simplification of this concept in terms Anne would understand would be like this: "Imagine that the Lake of Shining Waters was beautiful and without any fault; but hair dye was poured into it by free will. The Lake was now permeated with the dye and tainted anything it tried to clean. But Matthew, out of his great love for Anne emptied the lake by hand, scrubbed it clean, and filled it by himself with clean water from the brook that runs below Green Gables. Matthew did this for free—he didn't charge Anne a dime."

CHAPTERS 23-24
1. walk the ridgepole of Mr. Barry's kitchen roof
2. Marilla realized what Anne had come to mean to her. She now knew that Anne was dearer to her than anything else on earth.
3. 14 times
4. physical culture exercises
5. Miss Stacy said so
6. helping to pay for a schoolhouse flag

CHAPTERS 25-26
1. Anne was not dressed like the other girls.
2. shopping at William Blair's
3. twenty pounds of brown sugar and a garden rake
4. Mrs. Lynde making a dress for Anne with puffed sleeves
5. Anne wanted to feast her eyes on the dress.
6. a pair of the daintiest little kid slippers, with beaded toes and satin bows and glistening buckles
7. When Anne ran off the platform after the fairy dialogue one of her roses fell out and Gil picked it up and put it in his breast pocket.
8. because Josie Pye had told Bessie Wright that Julia Bell's bow when she got up to recite made her think of a chicken jerking its head, and Bessie told Julia
9. that a good moral was put in all the stories the girls wrote
10. Anne felt encouraged.

CHAPTERS 27-28
1. black hair
2. green hair
3. Anne's chatter
4. Anne's hair was ever so much darker than it used to be before it was cut.
5. Tennyson
6. A sharp stake at the landing had torn off the strip of batting nailed on the boat and the boat slowly sank.
7. Gilbert Blythe
8. Gilbert asked Anne to forgive him and be friends.
9. *The Amethyst Brooch Affair:*
   meddling with things that didn't belong to me
   The Haunted Wood:
   letting my imagination run away with me
   The Liniment Cake:
   carelessness in cooking
   The German Jew Dyeing:
   vanity
   Sinking of the Barry Flat:
   being too romantic
10. romance

ANNE OF GREEN GABLES
Answers

CHAPTERS 29-30

1. Charlotte's beau won't agree to that, because nobody ever has been married in the church yet, and he thinks it would seem too much like a funeral. *Church weddings were the norm for Anglicans but other Protestant denominations held weddings at home. In a later title Anne will be married "in the sunshine of the old orchard" and three years after* Anne of Green Gables *was first published, the author was married at home with only twenty guests present.*
2. Diana's mother had a letter from Aunt Josephine asking Diana and Anne to come to town and stop with her for the Exhibition.
3. because Marilla "doesn't intend to have Matthew going to Mrs. Lynde to make them."
4. homemade butter and cheese
5. to have a minister's wife for your friend
6. eating ice cream at a brilliant restaurant at eleven o'clock
7. Miss Barry generally laughed at anything Anne said, even when she said the most solemn things.
8. "the best of it all" was the coming home
9. She had an uneasy feeling that it was rather sinful to set one's heart so intensely on any human creature as she had set hers on Anne.
10. "She said we couldn't be too careful what habits we formed and what ideals we acquired in our teens, because by the time we were twenty our characters would be developed and the foundation laid for our whole future life. And she said if the foundation was shaky we could never build anything really worth while on it."
11. reading *Ben Hur*
12. to go to Queen's and study to be a teacher
13. "... because you are paid a salary for teaching, but a husband won't pay you anything, and growls if you ask for a share in the egg and butter money."
14. her feelings for Gilbert
15. Matthew had a bad spell with his heart and she didn't feel like leaving him.

Project 2

Dwight Lyman Moody was an American evangelist and publisher who founded the Moody Church, Northfield School and Mount Hermon School in Massachusetts (now the Northfield Mount Hermon School), the Moody Bible Institute and Moody Publishers.

Charles Haddon Spurgeon was a British Reformed Baptist preacher—the "Prince of Preachers." Spurgeon was a prolific author of many types of works including sermons, an autobiography, a commentary, books on prayer, a devotional, a magazine, and more.

CHAPTERS 31-32

1. because the Spencervale doctor instructed Marilla: "Keep that redheaded girl of yours in the open air all summer and don't let her read books until she gets more spring into her step."
2. Mrs. Lynde; because she keeps nagging people to do right
3. Anne said that she'd be able to study better because of her flounce and that she'd have such a comfortable feeling deep down in her mind about the flounce.
4. Anne said that it was nicer to think dear, pretty thoughts and keep them in one's heart, like treasures. She didn't like to have them laughed at or wondered over. And Miss Stacy said the short ones are much stronger and better.
5. "If you can't be cheerful, be as cheerful as you can."
6. He was repeating the multiplication table over and over.
7. She meant that success would be incomplete and bitter if she did not come out ahead of Gilbert Blythe.
8. because Anne and Gilbert *tied*
9. "You're a credit to your friends, Anne, that's what, and we're all proud of you."

CHAPTERS 33-34

1. The floor was covered with a pretty matting, and the curtains were of pale-green art muslin. The walls were covered with a dainty apple-blossom paper and a few good pictures. Miss Stacy's photograph occupied the place of honor with fresh flowers on the bracket under it. There was a white-painted bookcase filled with books, a cushioned wicker rocker, a toilet table befrilled with white muslin, and a quaint, gilt-framed mirror with chubby pink Cupids and purple grapes painted over its arched top.
2. Anne was going to recite for a concert at the White Sands Hotel.
3. that she is "just a dumpling"
4. Gilbert Blythe away at the back of the room, bending forward with a smile on his face
5. He said, "Who is that girl on the platform with the splendid Titian hair? She has a face I should like to paint."
6. She was thinking of the little girl Anne used to be

ANNE OF GREEN GABLES
Answers

and wishing she could have stayed a little girl (even with all her queer ways).
7. Gilbert
8. Beechwood was too far from the Academy.
9. to eat Marilla's cake
10. An Avery scholarship

CHAPTERS 35-36

1. Ruby Gillis (the handsomest girl of the year at the Academy)—She had large, bright-blue eyes, a brilliant complexion, and a plump showy figure. She laughed a great deal, was cheerful and good-tempered, and enjoyed the pleasant things of life frankly.
2. the "rose-red" girl, Stella Maynard, and the "dream girl," Priscilla Grant
3. Anne made Miss Barry love her. Miss Barry said, "I like people who make me love them. It saves me so much trouble in making myself love them."
4. chestnut buds and Maytime hazes
5. Anne was winner of the Avery.
6. Gilbert Blythe was going to teach, too. His father couldn't afford to send him to college so he intended to earn his own way through.
7. Matthew had some real bad spells with his heart and Marilla had a pain behind her eyes.
8. Abbey Bank was shaky.
9. Matthew said that he would rather have had Anne than a dozen boys.

CHAPTERS 37-38

1. the failure of the Abbey Bank
2. Anne's tearless agony
3. Marilla confessed her affection for Anne when she said, "I love you as dear as if you were my own flesh and blood and you've been my joy and comfort ever since you came to Green Gables."
4. To find pleasure in these things now that he has gone. Mrs. Allan understood. She told Anne, "We re-sent the thought that anything can please us when someone we love is no longer here to share the pleasure with us, and we almost feel as if we were unfaithful to our sorrow when we find our interest in life returning to us."
5. John Blythe was once Marilla's beau but they had a quarrel and Marilla wouldn't forgive him when he asked me to.
6. He told Marilla to give up all reading and sewing, not to cry, and if she wore the glasses he'd given her then Marilla's eyes might not get any worse and the headaches would be cured.
7. Duty. She had looked her duty courageously in the face and found it a friend—as duty ever is when we meet it frankly.
8. Anne decided to stay at home and teach instead of pursuing her education any further.
9. Gilbert withdrew his application to teach in Avonlea and suggested that they accept Anne's. He decided instead to teach at White Sands.
10. She told Gilbert that she forgave him that day by the pond landing and that she had been sorry ever since.
11. "Who was that came up the lane with you, Anne?"
12. "God's in his heaven, all's right with the world."

Anne's conclusion is a quote from Robert Browning's Pippa's Song:

> *The year's at the spring,*
> *And day's at the morn;*
> *Morning's at seven;*
> *The hill-side's dew-pearl'd;*
> *The lark's on the wing;*
> *The snail's on the thorn;*
> *God's in His heaven—*
> *All's right with the world!*

In the poem (of which this is only an excerpt), Pippa was an orphan girl who worked under terrible conditions. In the end she asserts that in spite all that is wrong in the world, we can still believe that God is there, and thus all is right with the world.